THE **TRUTH** BEHIND
TRUMP
DERANGEMENT
SYNDROME

There is more than meets the eye

John Fraser

Unless otherwise indicated, all Scripture quotations are taken from the New King James Version.
NLT (New Living Translation)

The Truth Behind Trump Derangement Syndrome
There is more than meets the eye

ISBN: 978-1-7329876-0-9

TABLE OF CONTENTS

INTRODUCTION

THE 2016 PRESIDENTIAL RACE has raised questions about what is going on. Why all the hysteria against Donald J. Trump? Why have things gotten so crazy in the political arena and the news? Sure, it has always been there to a degree, but the bar has really been raised. Why has the left gone way left? What's up?

Many are trying to explain why the left and the establishment have such hatred for President Trump. Some say it's because he is an outsider. Others say this and that, but there is more to this event.

Each chapter of this book will build a case that will undoubtedly show that there is more to what we can see with our natural eyes.

This book is not intended to destroy or hurt any persons or parties but merely to help make the reader aware to enhance his or her own knowledge.

It was written to show evidence that another realm truly exists in our midst while we live on planet Earth. Our lives will be directly affected in either a positive or a negative way depending on how well informed we are of this. If we are void of understanding, we can unwittingly be working against our own best interests.

In Colossians chapter one, it states that God wants us to be filled with the knowledge of His will in all wisdom and spiritual understanding.

If we do not believe in a spiritual realm, then we will be blind to our allies of light and the enemies of darkness.

If we do not believe in another realm, then we will not attempt to learn what is God's best for our lives.

To say there is no other realm is to say there is no God. For we know there is a God for His invisible attributes are clearly seen each and every day.

I pray that this book will enlighten your eyes and expose another perspective that will bring clarity to the times we are living.

CHAPTER 1

THE ANNOUNCEMENT

ON JUNE 16, 2015, while waiting at a traffic light in Farmingdale, New York, I heard Donald J. Trump announce his candidacy for president of the United States. I remember vividly the excitement I experienced not really understanding the full revelation of it.

Like many, I knew Mr. Trump as a wealthy businessman that was very successful in real estate, but I just knew that this was something bigger than his past victories.

Being a Christian, I perceived that this was a God thing and that he would be the next president of the United States. I didn't realize all he would have to endure to take that office.

I wasn't always a Christian even though I grew up going to a Christian school and church until my early adult years. In my twenties, I didn't have any spiritual understanding or connection to keep me going to church. I began to just go on the big holidays. Jesus just seemed like a Santa Claus figure at this point in my life.

I had zero spiritual awareness. The thing that I loved about Jesus was the holidays that came each year, but I never knew Him personally.

I had one of the best childhoods one could ever dream of. I was truly blessed with two loving parents, four brothers, and one sister. We all got along so well together and the holidays were such an amazing time as a child. Our parents magnified the Christmas and Easter holidays, and we just never wanted them to end.

But as time went on and we all began to grow up, one by one we began to leave the family nest and we all eventually stopped going to church on a regular basis.

For me, other things were more important and I didn't feel a need to go and hear the same thing over and over. It didn't seem to be teaching me anything about the daily things that I was dealing with. I felt like it was merely taking up one hour of my life each week, and I had nothing to show for it.

LIFE CHANGER

But at the age of thirty, at about 8 p.m. one evening, I opened up a Bible that hadn't been opened in years and read a random passage in the Gospel of John and then asked Jesus if He was real or not. Of course, He did say to us, "Seek and you will find," but I wasn't expecting what would happen next.

Within twelve hours, there was a gentleman talking to me about Jesus at a Dunkin Donuts, and he spoke about the same Scripture I had just read the night before. Was this a coincidence? Not a chance!

This was the beginning of my spiritual walk with God.

THE CALLING ON HIS LIFE

Back at the traffic light while pondering Donald Trump as president, I was reminded in a flash of a person in the Bible by the name of Jehu, who the prophet Elijah was commanded by God to anoint as the next king of Israel.

At this moment, I experienced a leap for joy in my spirit and I knew this was the Lord calling Donald Trump to step into the office as the next president.

This man Jehu in the Bible was a man with a serious attitude. I mean that in a good way. He was a man that didn't know what the word "compromise" was. He was a bold man and only took his coffee black. It had to be hot or just forget about it! I'm not really sure if he drank coffee but if he did, I'm sure it would have been bold and strong! He was a man that did things at full speed and never halfhearted. If he told you he would do something, he would do it without question. Whatever it took to get the job done, he would do it!

The Scriptures tell us that after Jehu was anointed to be the next king, that the commanders that were present there put their own garments under him at the top of the staircase where he was standing and they blew trumpets saying, "Jehu is king!"

Just like that, in just a moment of time, Jehu became the king of Israel. The people quickly supported him and rallied behind him. The ones that knew him closely didn't question his character or morals. They knew he was a man after God's heart and was passionate about his nation.

He wasted no time getting to work and headed toward a city called Jezreel while riding on a chariot. As he was still afar off, the watchmen of the city saw someone coming, but they didn't know it was Jehu approaching. But then, one recognized the way he was driving. For evidently, no one drove a chariot like Jehu did.

And the watchman said:

> **2 Kings 9:20**
> The driving is like the driving of Jehu the son of Nimshi, for he drives furiously!

We can see that Jehu stood out in a crowd by the way he drove his chariot. He drove fearlessly towards his enemies with boldness and confidence. He was like no other, for he immediately destroyed and overturned the unholy things in Israel and began to bring law and order to the land and hold the ones responsible for causing Israel to get into the condition they were now in.

Jezebel, the queen of Israel, did evil in the sight of the Lord and was the big reason for them leaving their heritage and godly ways. The Bible states that she worked her harlotry and witchcraft while she was in office and despised the way of righteousness. She was overthrown by Jehu, as some of her own eunuchs became whistleblowers, and turned her over to him to be judged and terminated.

Like Israel, America has fallen into all kinds of ungodly lifestyles without realizing it. A little here and a little there. America has been inundated with all sorts of unrighteous agendas under the radar. One by one, they crept into households through news outlets, social media, etc. and slowly began shaping a new way of living without much of a fight.

Now many have awakened to these radical liberal ways and now wonder how it got so bad. Many didn't see it coming. Many were sleeping on their watch. Many now wonder how things can be changed back.

As the days went forward, I began to realize the significance of why Donald Trump was chosen at this time to become our next president.

Like Jehu, Donald Trump doesn't have a first gear or second gear. He lives only in overdrive! He moves with purpose and precision and only knows one speed. Full speed! He drives furiously like Jehu and if he stays on course and doesn't lose focus, he will be used in a mighty way for America and our allies.

Washington has been filled with so many rats and swamp creatures for so long that it would take someone with a wrecking ball, a heart of steel, and more energy than the Energizer Bunny to get the job done.

Donald Trump would become our modern day Jehu, who would deliver America from the corrupt politicians that have weaseled their way into the undergrounds of our government. He was called to overthrow their agendas that now exist that would try to bring down our society.

If you look in the Old Testament, you will see so many stories how when Israel was in trouble that the people would cry out to the Lord and He would raise up a deliverer that would help save them or free them from bondage.

To name a few, He raised up David to take down the giant named Goliath and freed them from the Philistines. He raised up Moses to free the people from the hand of Pharaoh and led them out of Egypt, bringing them into the Promised Land.

Israel also had kings with evil hearts that were corrupt and did not follow the ways of their fathers and caused great sin in their land. And when they knew that things were going off track and their way of right living was in jeopardy, they cried out to the Lord.

Then God would hear their cries and raise up a deliverer who had a good and noble heart, one who loved the truth. Someone that would overturn the corruption and that would restore things back to law and order.

AMERICANS CRYING OUT

And just like Israel, America has elected men and women into office with liberal agendas and corrupt ways to change the way things previously were being done.

The people of God and the ones that understood spiritual truths saw what was happening and asked the Lord for a deliverer to change the course that America was on. To help restore the former days before the next generation has utterly taken over and the American way is dead.

My wife Nancy and I recognized things going south and off course. We knew it would take someone that was strong willed who could overcome all that has taken place in the last eight years under President Obama. We knew President

Obama spoke as one that claimed to be a Christian but was denying the Lord with many of his policies that he enforced with his signature. We knew he was not acting in the best interest of God's will for America.

We knew for the sake of our nation that we needed a deliverer to overturn many of the policies that have now been implemented into our society. We also understood that a strong America means stability for the entire world. America has rescued other nations from foreign leaders that have gone rogue over the years. The importance of having stiff pressure on Russia, China, North Korea, and Iran is essential in order to keep other nations in check.

America's existence and compassion is imperative for the survival of other nations. Of course, America hasn't been perfect but has been a beacon of hope for millions of people over the years.

THE PREPARATION

Everything up to this point in Donald Trump's life was just a preparation for what he was called to do! All the negotiating skills that he developed over the years in real estate were going to be used on a much larger scale than he could ever imagine.

All the knowledge of bidding on projects and keeping them under budget and ahead of schedule would play bigly for America's rebuilding ahead. Little did he know that in his latter days he would be called to the highest office in the country and to rule in the greatest nation on the planet.

After all those years of working and achieving the assets of a billionaire, he now would graciously lay down his career and his fortune and begin to work for the American people.

THE PACKAGE

His wife Melania and his family are all part of the package as well. They have been groomed for such a time as this. They are working on things that they have a compassion for and are making a big difference.

His relationship with his children is unquestionably wholesome and stable. It's refreshing to see a family speak so highly of one another and work together as one. You can easily discern the genuine love that they have for one another.

Jesus made this statement:

Matthew 7:18
A good tree cannot bear bad fruit,
nor can a bad tree bear good fruit.

Look at President Trump's children and look at the fruit he has produced. His children speak volumes about him as a man and a father. What a great testimony.

UPCOMING CHAPTERS

Books could be written for each one of the next chapters in this book. But for now, just the high points will be noted to help make you aware of the spiritual activities that are present in our society and to make known of the power of the gospel.

God in no way wants us to be ignorant of the spiritual forces at work on earth. He wants us to have a spiritual understanding so we will not be taken advantage of in any areas of our lives.

That's what the following Scripture tells us:

> **2 Corinthians 2:11**
> lest Satan should take advantage of us:
> for we are not ignorant of his devices.

The next chapters are not intended to make one afraid of the spiritual forces at work but to only expose them. And as one understands the authority God has given His Church, it will bring encouragement and it will empower them for the future. He has emphatically told us over and over again not to be afraid in any way but to learn the things He has provided for us.

CHAPTER 2

A MODERN DAY DELIVERER

AS THE DAYS ROLL on, the GOP nominees are piling in with a grand total of seventeen candidates that would be jockeying for the Republican nominee to be the next president of the United States.

Many of these names were well-known Christians with very good reputations. Names like Governor Mike Huckabee, Senator Ted Cruz, Senator Marco Rubio, Ben Carson, and so on.

The conservatives were very confused about whom to vote for. They had so many Christian leaders to choose from, but which one was the right one for the job?

It was frustrating to hear many believers and conservatives talk about whom they might vote for when I had the inside scoop already. Yes, many good candidates, for sure, and it seemed to some people that it was foolish to vote for Donald Trump since he wasn't a politician like we know. But what is God's best for such a time as this?

1 Corinthians 1:27 NLT
Instead, God deliberately chose things the world considers foolish in order to shame those who think they are wise.

America was at a crossroad and in a dire place. The Democrats, of course, didn't see it that way at all. On the contrary, they believed everything was wonderful and they couldn't afford to change anything.

We would need a modern day deliverer to set us free from the Washington D.C. creatures that were making it very difficult for America to reverse the damage they were doing internally.

Many liked Trump for his commanding presence and past ventures but weren't convinced because he seemed untamed like a wild stallion. He did, however, seem to know the affairs of the world for a man that was considered an outsider of the political arena. He always gave an answer that carried authority and depth to the questions that were asked of him. There was passion, zeal, and enthusiasm to destroy ISIS, build a wall, and bring back jobs to America.

God knew best for our nation, but the people of America would have to recognize we needed big help in a big way. We would need a person that was a hard nose who could oust the swamp machine and stop us from free falling. A commander and chief that had strong conservative agendas that could reverse the work that the former administration had implemented.

Conservative values will always create a society full of peace and good living. The evangelicals and the people of America had to vote for Donald Trump even if it didn't look right with their natural eye. God couldn't magically put him in office, for the American people ultimately would have to make that choice. God gave us a free will and would never mingle in the election process.

Many people believe God can do whatever He wants to do anytime He wants to do it, but that is definitely not the case. He is limited to what He is able to do. That might come as a surprise but it's the truth. He would like to be more involved in our everyday affairs, but we are the ones in control of that.

He wants to take our burdens, but most people either don't know that or they just want to do it themselves. He said to humble yourself and give Me your cares for I care for you. Look what it says in the Book of Peter:

1 Peter 5:6-7
Therefore humble yourselves under the mighty hand of God, that He may exalt you in due time, casting all your care upon Him, for He cares for you.

He wants us to cast our cares on Him and let Him have them.

Many people think they're the only ones that can get the job done, but if they would only humble themselves and look for His help, then they would find that things would work out much better and easier as well.

Now God is in control of heaven, where everything is perfect, but not here on the earth. If He were in control, we wouldn't have hundreds of babies being aborted every day. We wouldn't see crime and fraud around every corner.

God has made us in His image and likeness. He put us in charge to make the right decisions for our lives. If we would follow His advice, things would go much better here on planet Earth. But even when we make a mess of things, if we would pray and ask of Him, He would show us the way to victory!

Over the years, He used different vessels to deliver people from destruction and the likes, and the people He used were not perfect people by any means. If you look at the vessels He used, you might be amazed at their resumes. Moses had murdered a man and tried to cover it up. David did the same and had an adulterous affair with the wife of the man he had murdered. God won't find a perfect vessel but is looking for willing vessels to work through.

Donald Trump has flaws like all of us, but I do believe he has a willing heart to implement conservative and godly values in America. He has put aside all his personal fortunes and is running with all his might against every liberal institution that would try to impose its agendas on the America people.

He doesn't let Hollywood, the media, or the liberals slow him down. They have tried many tactics to divert him and control his actions, but he just continues to drive furiously yet so effortlessly through the swamp!

God is using President Trump as a modern day deliverer who will be a blessing to America and to the world! I believe "Making America Great Again" was on God's heart when He chose Donald Trump to help restore this nation back to the American values we once held.

Hold on and fasten your seat belts; we are in for a ride!

CHAPTER 3

WHY SO DERANGED?

WE KNOW THAT POLITICS has always been a heated subject but never have we seen the likes of this. The media has been ganging up on the president in a way that is unheard of. The left has been relentless in launching missile attacks at Donald Trump since he came on the scene. Why the hysteria and fake news? Why the resistance against every policy that he supports?

Conservative news outlets and contributors are scratching their heads trying to figure out why the radical left and other media outlets are completely against this president.

Everyone is trying to come up with all kinds of ideas of why they are making up stories every day about him. Is something else going on? Why would people be so opposed to this president?

THE INAUGURATION CEREMONY

How many of us can remember while Donald Trump was being sworn in as the forty-fifth president of the United States, that a woman down the street was in agony, screaming, "Noooo, noooo, noooo?"

Was this just one person's outcry of displeasure? Was this a normal reaction to being upset that your party lost? Why so enraged? Why did she seem so tormented and horrified?

Many people have chuckled after viewing this scene as if this was just some woman being a sore loser. It is sad to say, but this runs much deeper than that.

At the confirmation hearings of Judge Brett Kavanaugh, some of the people seated in the back of the room started shouting and screaming over the voices of some of the Republican senators while they were trying to speak. They acted deranged in nature as one by one they had to be led out of the room by security because of their behavior. This group, even though it was staged by the Democrats, seemed to be like mad dogs out of control.

And the day the senators were casting their vote for Brett Kavanagh in the Capitol Building, we heard the outcries from several individuals that were instructed beforehand that no one was allowed to say anything, yet they couldn't contain themselves from expressing the violence that burned in their souls.

After Judge Kavanagh's confirmation, we saw many people outside the Supreme Court trying to pound their way in with their fists like beasts. Why would people get so crazy about politics if that was all it was about?

Most people just believe that this is nothing more than people expressing their opinions and that they are just zealous people dedicated to their cause.

God wants us to believe that there is a spiritual realm. People always say they believe in God, but how can they believe in God and then they don't believe in a spiritual realm? He teaches us through His Word to look to the things that we cannot see with our physical eyes, because the things that we can only see with our natural eyes are only temporary and will not last.

> **2 Corinthians 4:18**
> while we do not look at the things which are seen, but at the things which are not seen. For the things which are seen are temporary, but the things which are not seen are eternal.

God wants us to know that there are things that you are not able to see with your natural eyes. The Word of God exposes the unseen realm and teaches us how to discern both good and evil. God warns us of spiritual hosts in this other realm that would like to cause us harm if we allow them.

Ephesians 6:12
For we do not wrestle against flesh and blood,
but against principalities, against powers, against
the rulers of the darkness of this age, against
spiritual hosts of wickedness in the heavenly places.

The Scripture is very clear and sheds light that people are not always the ones causing the problems we incur. Even though people might be carrying out the evil deed, a spiritual entity has provoked and motivated the action or attack.

That's why most problems people have with other people never really change much, because people are just trying to fix them by natural means and are not addressing the real root of the problem. People are just addressing the surface of the problem.

While I don't want you to think that everything that happens is because of darkness, and a devil is behind every door, the spiritual realm is the root of many of the problems people are having.

I believe we should never get into a ditch on one doctrine or another, but we need to learn how to walk in the middle of the road with God's truth. Many people have grabbed on to one truth of the Bible and went so extreme with that one truth that they are now living in a ditch. And that's why we have ended up with all these strange church doctrines and cults.

Now many people work so hard to make relationships work out, but they feel like they just keep hitting a brick wall. God's Word reveals that we're not always wrestling against flesh and blood but against these hosts of demonic forces. Our fight isn't against people but with spiritual powers influencing them. The majority are unaware of what is happening in the spirit and therefore waste much of their energy and life trying to put fires out that never seem to be extinguished.

Many are even taught that when challenging times come that God is behind it and that He has a reason for these things to happen. Religious leaders echo the same false teachings, which have a devastating effect on the ones looking for God's help.

God created us to dominate over every evil thing that would try to hurt us. He has given us everything we need to overcome. We just need to take the time and find out what He gave us.

God gets a bad rap and meanwhile, the Bible tells us that we are not dealing with flesh and blood but with spiritual darkness in the spiritual realm. God is for us and will never be against us. He is love and He sent His Son to rescue us. We need to get the story straight.

Too many people are mad at God for all the disasters in their lives and meanwhile, He is the One trying to help them the best He can! It is pertinent to know God and to know His ways. Most people just form a conclusion about why the things are happening based on what fits their fancy.

If you don't know who your enemy is, then your enemy will have a heyday with you. If God were your enemy, you would be fried up in a pan already. When you find out about this loving God and how He wants to help you, it's then you will begin to see breakthroughs in your life.

> **James 1:17**
> Every good gift and every perfect gift is from above, and comes down from the Father of lights, with whom there is no variation or shadow of turning.

The Father only knows how to bless us with good things and to love us like no one else can. When something happens that isn't good or isn't a blessing to us, we will know that it isn't God bringing it upon us. We can know for sure that you won't find His fingerprints on anything that would try to hurt us or hinder our lives.

UNHINGED

So as we look again at Ephesians chapter six, we can see one of the reasons why people are becoming unhinged and acting the way they are. It might not be politically correct to say, but according to what God's Word has to say, many are being energized by these powers of darkness to cause this resistance and divisions we see across America. Of course, these hosts of wickedness are not just using the liberals and certain Democrats as puppets to do their bidding but anyone that will yield to their anti-god agendas.

Before I go to the next chapter, I first would like to share a story that opened my eyes to this spiritual realm that we are now discussing. Since this event, I have experienced many other times of seeing spiritual activity while being wide awake.

In 1990, I had just become a Christian and I didn't know much of what the Scriptures said. One night, I was just getting into bed and my spiritual eyes were open. Suddenly I saw an evil spirit in my room. I just ran out of the room in fear and turned all the lights on.

I told one of my brothers what I had seen the next day and he said if you see it again just say the name of Jesus. Well, I saw it again not too long after that first experience and I almost ran out of my room again in fear but this time, I just looked at it for about five seconds and then I stuttered the word "Jesus" out of my mouth. I was so terrified that it took everything to get His name out.

But like a flash, it was gone. I knew at that moment that I didn't need to be afraid of it happening again because I had the answer. The answer was His name! What a discovery.

As I studied the Scriptures, I found that every believer could use His name when encountering problems in their life. Jesus told His followers to use His name whenever they needed to.

The Bible tells us that His name carries authority and power. I'm so glad I found this great truth out for I won't live a day without Him in my life.

Look what this Scripture informs us:

Ephesians 1:20-21
which He worked in Christ when He raised Him from the dead and seated Him at His right hand in the heavenly places, far above all principality and power and might and dominion, and every name that is named, not only in this age but also in that which is to come.

The Bible tells us that after Jesus was raised from the dead, His Father made His name to be higher and greater than any other name.

Philippians 2:10
that at the name of Jesus every knee should bow, of those in heaven, and of those on earth, and of those under the earth

Paul states:

Ephesians 1:22-23
And He put all things under His feet, and gave Him to be head over all things to the church, which is
His body...

If you can get a hold of this, it will really be a blessing to you. It states that the Father put all things under Jesus' feet and Jesus is the head of the Church and the Church is His body.

So that potentially gives a member of His Church the right to use His name and to put whatever is bothering them under their feet.

Unfortunately, most in the Church are not taught these truths and therefore even though they have a right to use His name, they don't because no one told them or they haven't read it for themselves.

Anyone who believes in Him automatically has the right to use His name. It doesn't matter what church you go to. It doesn't matter how spiritual you are. You might not think you are much, but His name is even given to the little pinky toe on His foot. All things were put under His feet!

This concludes that His name is the greatest name of all! Jesus!

CHAPTER 4

THE SYNDROME

MANY IN OUR NATION have seemed to be contaminated with an affliction called the Trump Derangement Syndrome. Once a person has been infected by this affliction, they can't seem to say anything good about President Trump.

It doesn't matter if he helps protect them from terrorists, or if he saves them hundreds of dollars on their taxes. It doesn't matter what good things he does for them, they just can't seem to say one pleasant thing about him.

In fact, they just can't seem to help themselves from making up false accusations and saying all sorts of vile things about him. Has someone hypnotized these people? Has their drinking water been poisoned with toxic anti-Trump serum? Who has done this thing to them?

How can they think so badly of a man who stands for law and order? A person that does what he says he will do. An American that loves our nation and veterans, and makes peace with other nations through strength. A man that works to bring jobs back to the American people and break records for unemployment and the stock market.

Why hate the greatest negotiator on the planet when he is making great deals for us? Where is the "love trumps hate" they so often declare? Yet they show such a hatred for a man that's working for the forgotten men and women in this nation. Something does not add up here.

Is there an antidote to reverse this syndrome that has plagued so many in this nation?

THE DARK SIDE

The human side of us seems to gravitate to the dark side and tends to be fascinated with evil spirits and ghosts. We seem to be intrigued with the dark side of things in our humanity rather than the God side of things.

Many of our youth love expressing darkness by their apparel and black wardrobes, which can be meant to represent death. They proudly flaunt their many figures of skulls and all types of demonic images.

Unfortunately, this is not just some innocent phase in their lives that they are going through. Why the deep hunger to follow after everything that stands against life and goodness? Are they following someone or is it just a passion that they were born with? Many run to see mediums and gypsies in hopes of getting some insight to what the future might bring them.

Halloween has always been a big holiday where I live, but we now have the chainsaw massacre and the living dead on the front lawns of several homes in our neighborhood. The decorations are so graphic and gruesome that I'm surprised parents would even bring their children to these houses to trick or treat. No joke, they are enough to give kids and adults nightmares and I'm sure they do.

I remember the simple decorations that our family would put out at our house on Halloween. They are no contest to these bloody and gory images that are on display today.

I understand that people for the most part are just wanting to make things fun. But think about this for a moment – why is this fun and exciting? Why are skeletons, blood, and death exciting to many? You won't find any of these gory images displayed in heaven, so why do most people enjoy manifesting fear and death?

I live not too far from the Amityville Horror house and I sure wish I had a nickel for every person that I saw taking a selfie in front of the house. People are constantly passing by every day to come and see this landmark where a family was brutally murdered. Many believe it's a haunted house. Why are humans running to see this house?

Many times when I call to place an order by phone and give my shipping address, and they hear Amityville as my town, they begin to ask questions about this house. Their voice changes to a whisper as they want to get some inside information about this mystical house.

It just so happens that my older brother went to school with one of the young girls that was murdered many years ago. That was a tragic night, indeed. Also, one of my son's friends lived in the house recently for quite some time.

People would ask me if demons were really in the house and if they were involved in the murder. Sure they were, but the demons were working through the one carrying out this horrible deed. It's not the house that's the problem – it's always the person being used.

People come to see this house from all over and yet the house has nothing to do with it. I'm sure Hollywood has probably given that impression, but evil spirits are everywhere.

From my observation, the majority of people would rather talk and seek demonic activity than witness angelic and godly activity.

Most Hollywood producers would rather make a horror movie rather than a clean family movie because they know there is a big audience for murder and violence. Our society has a desire for blood and murder more than a good wholesome family program. Hollywood produces what sells. They produce what the people desire and it fills their pockets with cash.

Why do we see books like Harry Potter and sorcery flying off the bookshelves? Why do the masses of people love to look on death and follow its path?

We were all born with a spiritual knowing that God is alive and that He does truly exist. Some may think that isn't true, but through our daily activities of life, most of us did not retain this awareness of God nor desired to pursue His way.

In the Book of Romans, it states that God has made Himself known to us, but many have suppressed His existence.

> **Romans 1:20**
> For since the creation of the world His invisible attributes are clearly seen, being understood by the things that are made, even His eternal power and Godhead, so that they are without excuse

He has shown even His eternal power and Godhead. Through teachings of evolution and the likes, many have used it as an excuse to do things their way, but deep down they know that God does exist.

You never hear anyone cry, "Oh my monkey," when they are in distress, but you do hear people cry, "Oh my God."

Most of us have become a product of the teachings of Hollywood, the media, and the spiritually uninformed, which has led us into all kinds of ungodly ways of living rather than living the life that God intended us to live.

DARKNESS AND THE LIGHT

Whatever side you choose to participate with, that side will impact the way you think and your thoughts will impact your actions.

Whatever side you yield to and obey, the greater the influence darkness or light will move in your life.

Romans 6:16
Do you not know that to whom you present yourselves slaves to obey, you are that one's slaves whom you obey, whether of sin leading to death, or of obedience leading to righteousness?

The greater desire for the side we choose to look upon will be the greater passion we will have for that side.

The Scripture states to whom you obey you are that one's slave. This is a powerful statement. Whatever path people are walking on that is the path they have become a slave to. The reason we as humans have a hard time changing bad habits and keep sinning in the same area is that it's not a natural thing we are dealing with. We have become a slave of unrighteousness and it will need to be dealt with on a spiritual level.

ADDICTIONS

In today's society, we treat addictions as a disease. Most doctors believe certain chemicals in the mind have triggered different nerves that now have altered their habits and behaviors.

When we think of addictions, we think maybe of an alcoholic or a smoker. We say that the alcohol they were drinking is addictive and now they can't stop drinking it because of its addicting properties. And a smoker now is addicted to nicotine because of its addicting power.

But what about someone that is addicted to gambling? Was it the dice that they were throwing that has addicting powers that now is controlling them? What about someone addicted to pornography? Are those magazine pages made out of some type of material that has addicting power?

Of course not. The problem stems from people participating with it and acting upon it too long. The same goes for playing video games on our computers or phones. We in a sense have made it our master and now we are slaves of it.

Many of those that have eating disorders were trying to lose weight but fell into extremism and now even though they are so thin, they have become a slave to losing more weight.

From the Scripture that we just read, we have given it power to rule over us. God didn't do it, Mama didn't do it, but we did it to ourselves.

Romans 6:16
you are that one's slaves whom you obey, whether of sin leading to death, or of obedience leading to righteousness?

People try to blame their problems in many cases on someone else. But leaning too far to the dark side will cause addictions and the likes.

ACTIVIST AND EXTREMIST

This explains how we have so many extreme groups in the world so passionate about their cause. They have become a product of the very thing they have indulged in.

They have chosen ungodly agendas and they played with it for too long. They gave too much of their attention to anti-god theology and it became truth to them. It has now become a way of life to them and no one can seem to straighten them out with good old fashion common sense. It seems to just irritate them even more.

Try to have a civil discussion with one of them and steam starts to erupt from their nostrils. It's their way or no way.

They now have become addicted to the war against President Trump. They are overtaken with bad thoughts about him and they don't seem capable of giving him any credit for the good he is doing.

They think they are at war with the president but in reality, they are against the things of God. Just look at what this president stands for. He stands for prosperity, freedom, peace, the family, health, education, and the life of every child in a mother's womb.

Because they have chosen to follow anti-god agendas and have indulged themselves in these political issues, they now have become a slave to them and will do anything and everything to have what they desire and whatever they think they need.

Just like a person who is addicted to something, they have become deceived and cannot seem to see what has happened.

The media has been allies with the Democratic Party for years not because of their love for one another but because they too have embraced radical thinking and have become captured to do the Devil's bidding as well.

We are seeing many in the mainstream media today that have opened themselves up to these things and now have wrong thinking and an evil mindset.

Whatever the president decides is good for the nation, we see people flipping out over good policies. For example, when President Trump speaks about immigration, they fight him tooth and nail. They used to be for keeping immigration laws to a certain degree, but now they have gone as far as wanting to get rid of ICE to enforce immigration and criminal activity.

Whatever the president wants now, they are against it. They will not agree on anything with this president. The media and the liberals look pretty foolish at some of the things they are complaining about.

Why would you want open borders? Why would you abolish ICE? Why have sanctuary cities? Why would you want higher taxes? Why would you want socialism when it doesn't work? They are looking very foolish at the moment and they don't even know it.

Some have said that Jesus doesn't believe in borders. But He said no man comes to the Father except through Me. Heaven has a gate and has a border. No one can enter heaven without going through Him. He also mentioned that He is the door.

John 10:9
I am the door. If anyone enters by Me, he will be saved...

So no one will be able to illegally enter heaven without doing it the proper way. Jesus says, "I am the way."

So we can see from the Scriptures that people will become addicted to whatever they participate in. You cannot play with fire and not get burned.

The hatred for this president is not warranted. Of course, I do realize he has made some mistakes in his past, but who hasn't? I also understand that he can sound a little rough around the edges at times, but that's not the cause for this revolution we see against him.

They proclaimed that they didn't like him because of his offensive tweets and that he isn't very presidential, but they have shown that it really isn't the reason.

They even flipped out on Judge Kavanaugh's nomination well before some women came forward with their accusations. The man had an unbeatable track record from his previous years serving as a judge. They threw everything and the kitchen sink at him to try to stop him as well.

Their real concern wasn't that he might have done something wrong but that he stands for things that are right! They know he is a conservative and that's why they objected from the very beginning.

The hearings turned into a three-ring circus as they tried to defame this man and have him cast out as Supreme Court judge. Most Americans saw this first hand and were mortified at the treatment this man received.

Something must be going on to have such hatred for an American that has served his country with dignity. Some even stated that "they were finished" if Kavanaugh were to get this position because he is for the life of babies and will turn over their abortion rights.

A COMPROMISING LIFE

The majority of people are in the middle of the road. They choose to partake of a little darkness and a little of light all depending on which day of the week it is.

Sitting on the fence between darkness and light puts people in a mediocre state in their lives. It's a compromising lifestyle of wishy washy people. It's an unstable and vulnerable place to live.

Even though most of us are not extremists, we still have a master in our lives. Jesus said that no man could have two masters.

Matthew 6:24
No one can serve two masters; for either he will hate the one and love the other, or else he will be loyal to the one and despise the other...

Find out how NOT to become a slave and how to be free of any unhealthy addictions. Much is at stake. We need to get off the fence and search out God's plans for America and our lives.

CHAPTER 5

AN ARMY MERGING AS ONE

WE ARE SEEING AN unprecedented hoard of unrighteous activists and extremists coming together as one. Darkness seems to have gathered all these different rebellious groups into one army.

They had been scattered into different platoons, but now in these days they have formed an allegiance with one another under the same umbrella. (Immigrant groups, anti-ICE groups, feminist groups, gender groups, atheist groups, globalist groups, etc.)

Their groups go by the name of division, fear, lies, and intimidation. They always try to divide our country by these tactics. They paint a narrative about the conservative groups and twist the truth, constantly spreading lies about the ones that are standing for truth and righteousness. They sow their seeds of discords and lies.

The leaders of this army incite riots and violent protests across our nation. The leaders inform their followers to cause havoc. We see the liberal leaders blatantly calling on their followers to go out and get in the face of our governing officials to stop them from implementing any conservative agendas.

In the meantime, liberal news outlets are working in harmony with these extremists by spewing false propaganda against the president and any person that will stand for godly principles.

This liberal attitude and behavior have been around since the beginning of Man but are today manifesting in an even greater way. This phenomenon is not limited to only America, but we see these outcries in all parts of the world.

These people are passionate about what they now believe in. These ideals seemed to have given them a purpose in life. They seem to have formed a bond with one another. Social media has indeed helped them to grow in numbers and has helped to expand their base.

Let's look in Proverbs:

Proverbs 14:12
There is a way that seems right to a man,
but its end is the way of death.

They seem to be convinced that their way is the right way and the only way, but do not see what road they are on. When people are not educated or informed, they will fall into the same error of the wicked.

Peter says:

> **2 Peter 3:17**
> You therefore, beloved, since you know this beforehand, beware lest you also fall from your own steadfastness, being led away with the error of the wicked;

There is a way of the wicked, which is in error and it wants us to believe it's the right and only way. Jesus tells us how to avoid going the wrong way and how to go the right way. He states that He is the way and the truth and the life. If we will humble ourselves and follow Him, we will not go the way of the wicked and crash and burn!

Most of the Democrats' agendas are in direct conflict with God's agendas. When you see this as a spiritual battle, then your eyes will be open to more of the truth. Destroying God's principles that this country was founded on is Satan's plan.

Satan knows that Donald Trump is the real deal. He endeavors to work different strategies to put down the president and paint a false narrative about him through those that will yield to him.

Many are in full attack mode coming at him with everything they have in their arsenal. The president is absolutely blowing their minds. Nothing seems to faze him. He keeps plowing forward with amazing grace. The productivity he has produced while in office for such a short period is like nothing we have seen.

Is Donald Trump perfect? Of course not, and none of us are but he stands up for righteousness and truth. This is the main reason we are seeing people becoming unhinged at the seams and we are witnessing them having fits of rage before our eyes.

When anyone stands for godly principles like Judge Kavanaugh and applies to one of the highest seats of power (Supreme Court), you will have a big fat target on your back. The last thing the Devil wants is a God-fearing person taking the office of the Supreme Court.

Jesus said that when you stand up for righteousness' sake you would be persecuted.

2 Timothy 3:12
Yes, and all who desire to live godly in Christ Jesus will suffer persecution.

He is basically saying it comes with the territory. If you follow Him and live a godly life, then know you will experience resistance and people coming against you. And the spirit realm is the root cause of these attacks but He warns us not to grow weary but to stand strong in Him and continue.

> **Matthew 10:22**
> And you will be hated by all for My name's sake. But he who endures to the end will be saved.

Here Jesus says that you will be hated for His name's sake. That doesn't just happen naturally. People seem to never take into account the spiritual principles that Jesus often spoke about. There is a force against Him and any that would later follow His Word and ways. Look what happened after the apostles were beaten for teaching in Jesus' name:

> **Acts 5: 40-41**
> and when they had called for the apostles and beaten them, they commanded that they should not speak in the name of Jesus, and let them go. So they departed from the presence of the council, rejoicing that they were counted worthy to suffer shame for His name.

They rejoiced that they suffered for His name's sake. Why would they rejoice? Because they understood these were spiritual attacks and He was well worth any punishment that they would ever endure. He laid His life down for them and gave them eternal life and now in turn they were willing to lay their life down for Him.

You will never be able to figure spiritual things out with your head. You have to begin to read God's Word and trust Him with your heart. It's then the eyes of your heart will be enlightened and you will begin to know the hope of His calling for your life.

John 6:63
The words that I speak to you are spirit, and they are life.

CHAPTER 6

WORKING FOR SATAN

PEOPLE THINK THAT BECAUSE they're not engaged with Ouija boards or satanic rituals that they're not participating in any of the Devil's games. But I have shocking news for you. We have all participated in darkness at certain times in our lives to some degree.

I understand that no one wants to think that this is even possible, but if we let the Scriptures teach us the truth, it has the power to transform our lives.

Look at what the apostle Paul tells the believers in Ephesus:

> **Ephesians 2:1-3**
> And you He made alive, who were dead in trespasses and sins, in which you once walked according to the

> course of this world, according to the prince of the power of the air, the spirit who now works in the sons of disobedience, among whom also we all once conducted ourselves in the lusts of our flesh, fulfilling the desires of the flesh and of the mind, and were by nature children of wrath, just as the others.

Paul is telling believers that before they had their sins washed away, they were dead in their sins. And while they were uninformed and blind spiritually, they walked in darkness and did things according to the prince of the power of the air.

It says that this spirit is still working in the sons of disobedience right now. That is why many are dumbfounded by the outrageous remarks that come from some of the very educated people of our day.

This Scripture helps us to see why we might be seeing some of the crazy things that are going on in Washington and around America today.

Many do not realize that Satan's mission is to stop anything associated with godly principles. This president has a bigger heart for God's agendas and His ways than most people know.

Many people and even Christians do not see this part of him because they are side tracked by his personality and by his bold statements.

He is accomplishing more for the kingdom of God than people really understand. Five days after taking office, President Trump signed an executive order banning overseas groups that received federal funding from spreading information about abortion. This president is pro-life and pro-God.

He has put two conservative judges into the Supreme Court that stand up for godly principles. He has moved the embassy to Jerusalem to show his support for the people of Israel.

He wasn't going to allow "Merry Christmas" to be substituted with "Happy Holidays," and many other such things he is so passionate about. Even though his outward man might not always show a Christ-like appearance, his inner man has Him in his heart and stands up for Him in his agendas. That is something that many are not picking up under the radar.

Most people think God is not interested in politics. That He is concerned just with the simple things in life and He doesn't pay too much attention to what is happening in Washington and things concerning our government.

That is so far from the truth. If you look back in the Old Testament, the Bible is filled with the stories of each king that ruled in those days. The kings were noted for their devotion for godly principles or their disobedience and wicked ways.

And if that king was wicked and had an evil heart, that nation went off into sin and had many issues in their lives. But the kings that honored God and His Word saw prosperity and blessings trickling down to the people and that nation.

God knows that if a king will stand up for truth and godly agendas, then that nation will be blessed. Just like a large corporation, if the head of a corporation is no good and has ungodly policies, then there will be all sorts of problems that will develop throughout the company's existence unless someone with good policies takes over at the helm.

In fact, two of the books in the Bible are called First Kings and Second Kings. God has always paid attention to kings and leaders from the beginning because He knows much is at stake for the people that are under their ruler ship.

Do you think God has any personal feelings about our nation's abortion rights or other policies that have a huge effect on people's lives? God does care about them because He cares about us.

As a child, I always heard you shouldn't talk about religion or politics, and now I understand why, because they touch the very core of our beliefs and spirit.

STOP WORKING FOR HIM

Now just because someone believes in Jesus, it doesn't mean they are immune to following this prince of darkness known as Satan. The way you begin to stop following his lifestyle is to become a disciple of Jesus and follow after Him. As we learn His Word and His ways, we won't be easily moved to act according to this prince as before.

Jesus said, "My sheep know My voice and will not listen to a stranger." Wow, what a statement! He is telling us that we can know His voice and will not follow a stranger like Satan.

Of course, we still have to make the choice to either yield to walking in darkness or walking Christ-like.

Learning to hear His voice and follow Him doesn't come overnight. It is a process and we will still make mistakes and fall into different sins along our journey, but we have to just keep getting back up and do what we know to do.

God designed the church for just that process but, unfortunately, most churches are not designed to disciple or teach His Word.

Many people have been going to church for years yet do not know these Scriptures that we are discussing. Many are not learning how they can be an overcomer and live a victorious life. Instead, many are still being victimized because for a lack of understanding. We have to read what His Word says and then it will make us free.

John 8:32
And you shall know the truth,
and the truth shall make you free.

Church is not a place that we appease our conscience and put our one hour in. It's a place for us to learn about Him and find out what His plan is for our lives. Many people believe if they go to church that they will be rewarded and go to heaven.

That's one of the biggest deceptions of religion. Many religious institutions do not teach people about salvation but are taught to make sure to go to church and give in the offerings.

When you tell people they have to go to church, it instills a work mentality in order to go to heaven. All religions of the world teach that you must do something or you have to abstain from something and then you will be rewarded for your good deeds.

I've had the opportunity to pray with many elderly people while they were in their last days. I would ask them if they think they will go to heaven when they pass on from this life.

Before you read on, ask yourself the same question. Will you have access to heaven when you pass on from this life?

I would say that eighty percent of the time people would answer me in a similar fashion. They would tell me, "Yes, because I've belonged to so and so church and I've always tried to do the best I could. I never hurt anyone intentionally. God knows my heart."

As explained earlier, I grew up going to church and I even became an altar boy, but what did that do for me? Does going to church make you a Christian? Does doing the best you can give you access to heaven? To most people, the answer would be yes.

If this was all true, then what in the world did Jesus come down from heaven for? And why did He die a violent death on that cross? Why didn't He just tell us to do the best we can?

It's tragic that many have not heard the truth of salvation. Many good people never hear what God has provided for them and they're unaware of how to receive it.

SALVATION

Salvation is not what you have done, but what God has done.

No man or woman can earn salvation on their own. We all have sinned and have fallen short. We all need a Savior.

Look what Paul said:

> **Philippians 3:9**
> and be found in Him, not having my own righteousness, which is from the law (works), but that which is through faith in Christ, the righteousness which is from God by faith;

Our righteousness and good works will never be good enough. We have to receive God's righteousness. I know some people think they might be good enough but think again. We all have sinned and without a Savior, we are wretched like the song Amazing Grace states.

His righteousness is a free gift but even though it's free, it doesn't just fall on us. We have to be willing to receive this great gift.

Jesus said:

John 3:16
For God so loved the world that He gave His only begotten Son, that whoever believes in Him should not perish but have everlasting life.

He said you have to believe it! Not just hear about it. You have to receive God's Son Jesus by faith.

And this is how you do it:

Romans 10:9
that if you confess with your mouth the Lord Jesus and believe in your heart that God has raised Him from the dead, you will be saved.

Another Scripture states:

> **Romans 10:13**
> For "whoever calls on the name of the Lord
> shall be saved."

The Father sent Him on behalf of you and me. Jesus paid the price for our sins. That was the purpose of His coming to earth.

If you want to receive this awesome gift, then you just need to tell the Father that you believe in His Son Jesus whom He sent and open your heart and receive Him. And when you do that, every sin from the past will be gone and His Spirit will come into you and then you'll have eternal life with Him. It is a spiritual experience! It's not a religious ritual. You will be born of His Spirit and then you have access to heaven.

So if you prayed that prayer and then someone asks you if you were going to heaven when you died, the answer would be, "Yes!" Why? Because I believe Jesus died for me. Period! No more bragging about ourselves. Nothing about what we did but only about what He did.

He took our sins away.

> **Ephesians 2:8-9**
> For by grace you have been saved through faith, and
> that not of yourselves; it is the gift of God, not of works,
> lest anyone should boast.

CHAPTER 7

MIND GAMES

WHAT I'M ABOUT TO explain is not a theory, but a fact. God's Word teaches us that Satan is the ultimate magician and master of disguise. He hides himself while working behind the scenes. The Bible describes him as a deceiver.

> **Revelation 12:9**
> So the great dragon was cast out, that serpent of old, called the Devil and Satan, who deceives the whole world; he was cast to the earth, and his angels were cast out with him.

How does he deceive us? Well, Jesus tells us that he is the father of lies and he works his lies through our thought life. The Bible explains that he plays mind games with us. His diabolical plan is for us to receive his thoughts without him being exposed.

The Devil operates under the radar like stealth without being noticed. He whispers his thoughts like seeds over our minds and desires us to allow them to take root in our hearts.

If his thoughts are not rejected, they will begin to germinate inside us. They will shape and mold us without us realizing it. They will have a direct impact on the things we stand for and they will have a lasting effect on our behaviors.

The Bible tells us to cast down imaginations and every thought that would try to rise above what God says.

2 Corinthians 10:5
Casting down imaginations, and every high thing that exalteth itself against the knowledge of God, and bringing into captivity every thought...

Most people believe that every thought that comes to their mind was from their mind.

The origin of a thought is paramount to not being deceived and influenced by the dark side. Once you understand this simple truth about the battle for our minds, it will revolutionize your life.

The Scripture tells us that we need to take each thought and bring it into captivity. It warns us to examine our thoughts and to judge each one of them.

HEAVEN OR HELL

Let me give you an example of this over in Matthew chapter sixteen. This will clearly show how we can be influenced by heaven or by hell.

Jesus asked His disciples this question, "Who do you say that I am?" Peter said, "You are the Christ, the Son of the living God." Jesus replied, "Flesh and blood has not revealed this to you, but My Father in heaven."

In other words, a thought came to Peter from heaven and revealed that Jesus was the Son of God. Jesus told him that it was His Father in heaven that gave him that information.

Notice Jesus said flesh and blood has not revealed this to you. What a revelation! Our thoughts are not just our brain organically manufacturing logical information. We can be receiving thoughts from heaven as well.

After that, Jesus begins to tell His disciples that He will suffer many things by the Scribes and that he will be killed. After He said that, Peter took Jesus aside and rebuked Him and said that this will not happen to Him. Jesus turned from Peter, and said, "Get behind Me, Satan."

Can you believe what just happened? Jesus recognized that Peter was now influenced by Satan with a thought, and He refused to receive a lie. He immediately rebuked Satan and wasn't going to receive what Peter had spoken to Him.

What a huge lesson for us! Not only was Peter influenced by heaven but just minutes later, he was influenced by hell. Peter yielded to both thoughts that he picked up in his mind and didn't stop to think where they had come from.

That is exactly what most people do. They just say what they think. That is very dangerous. Unfortunately, we all have said things without stopping to think where the thought came from. That's why the Bible says to be "slow to speak." (James 1:19)

Satan uses people to redirect others from doing what they ought to do. In this case, he was using Peter to try to change Jesus' plans. So many people had dreams of what they felt was good to do but instead listened to someone that instructed them to go another route. Satan has used all of us to a certain degree, and if we are not careful and slow to speak, he will use us again.

We can see from these Scriptures that if we receive advice, even from friends and family, that it might not be God's best. In fact, it could be coming from a source that is trying to steer us in the wrong direction.

They might love us and may be very sincere, but we still have to follow and watch the words spoken over us. Peter loved

Jesus and didn't mean Him any harm, yet he yielded to the thoughts of Satan and spoke them. Jesus discerned that Peter unfortunately became a messenger for Satan and renounced what he had spoken over Him.

We need to, so to speak, put a filter on what we think. If we don't and we just welcome every thought to have space in our minds, then we will be subject to wrong thinking about many things and will be like Peter and give our loved ones wrong advice instead of sound wisdom.

WHAT ARE YOU THINKING?

There is one that wants us to think wrongly, but God wants us to think right. If we think on wrong thoughts, we will have all kinds of anxieties and fears that will torment us. You just can't think on what comes to your mind without it causing major disasters. Suicide and the likes are all associated with this truth.

To illustrate this point, there are many radio waves in our presence, but we cannot see them with our physical eyes. They can only be heard if we pick them up with a radio receiver.

Our minds are like spiritual receivers. There are many spiritual stations out there jockeying for us to tune into their station and receive their thoughts. There's the good, the bad, and the ugly.

The broadcasts that we participate with the most will have a greater influence in our lives. Those broadcasts will be able to speak more into us and help shape our habits and ways for the good or the bad.

When one enjoys the unrighteous and perverted conversations of the world, that one is susceptible to receiving Satan's broadcasts of deceptions and lies into their minds.

It's a slow process but over time, it transforms one to be an extremist for the kingdom of darkness.

Many have opened themselves up to the nonsense that we are seeing today because they have loved unrighteousness and they have hated the truth.

The liberals seem to be lying about so many things and their logic doesn't seem to make sense or add up. Just like we see how Peter was used by Satan, many politicians are being used as puppets and do not know it.

Now let's not forget what the Scripture states. It states to cast down imaginations and everything that exalts itself or elevates itself higher than what God says.

If you do not know what God says, then how will you distinguish if a thought is from God or Satan? If a thought is from heaven or hell? You must find the truth so you are not deceived and lied to any longer. It's as simple as that!

Many people live with all kinds of fears because of this reality. People go to doctors and take medication to try to relieve their minds and have found some peace. If they would believe this truth and start reading what God says about them, then they could begin to combat those lies with the truth and turn things around in their lives. It starts by tuning into the truth and tuning out the junk.

Here is an example of God's thoughts toward us:

Psalms 139:13
For You formed my inward parts;
You covered me in my mother's womb.

Verses 17-18 - How precious also are Your thoughts to me, O God! How great is the sum of them! If I should count them, they would be more in number than the sand; When I awake, I am still with You.

God is absolutely crazy about us. He is in love with us. Once you begin to know the thoughts God has for you and what He says about you, then when wrong thoughts come to your mind, you will begin to distinguish where they came from. Not only will this help you live a peaceful life, but it will also lead you in the way you should go.

God has given us His manual to live a successful life. Jesus said that His Word is living and powerful. The Bible is dead and useless to only those that think it's dead and useless. It will breathe life into you if you open it in faith.

If you have never read the Bible, I would recommend you start at the Gospel of John. That's a good place to begin, and then get into a church that opens their Bible and teaches from it.

Pray and ask God to help you to find a good church that will develop you and make you a strong disciple of Jesus. So, when the storms of life come, you will not be moved nor be afraid.

Look what this famous Scripture in Psalms 23 tells us:

Psalms 23:4
Yea, though I walk through the valley of
the shadow of death, I will fear no evil;
For You are with me;
Your rod and Your staff, they comfort me.

The rod and staff is referring to the Word of God. And when we get a hold of His Words, then we will not be afraid when evil times arise in our lives. That "shadow of death" will not scare us like it used to. Fear won't affect us like it once did. Knowing the truth and knowing He is with us, changes everything!

These things are key to seeing your life changed. So start to feed on His thoughts and ways today and watch how God's peace will surround you and keep you.

CHAPTER 8

THY WILL BE DONE

WE ARE LIVING IN an unprecedented time in our history. As we've noted, there is a cause for all this hostility we are witnessing today.

Man has been inspired by hosts of evil angelic beings to rebel against the things of God. When you think it can't get any crazier, think again. Protestors and violent groups have been well organized and funded by several persons and institutions to disrupt the American way.

HEAVEN ON EARTH

The disciples asked Jesus to teach them to pray. He gave them the prayer that we have so infamously named the Our Father. And in this prayer, He reveals that God's kingdom has come and that His will shall be done on earth as it is in heaven. This is awesome news! This is God's will! He wants the things that are going on in heaven to be happening here on the earth.

> **Matthew 6:9-10**
> In this manner, therefore, pray:
> Our Father in heaven, Hallowed be Your name.
> Your kingdom come.
> Your will be done on earth as it is in heaven.

The Father's will is for us to live in health, prosperity, and have love for one another. He wants us to walk in peace and joy each and every day.

He doesn't want us to be partakers of riots, violence, hatred, and the likes that we are seeing today. Division and false accusations are a way of life here and it's not His will.

An enemy has stirred up many oppressive dictators and many other leaders to keep this earth from having days of heaven on the earth.

There are some in the Democratic Party that have veered off their long-standing policies and agendas and have gone rogue and way to the left of their traditional values.

It was God's original plan for earth to be like heaven, but temptations gave birth to sin and now we are living in what the Bible calls a fallen world.

If God's will is for earth to be like heaven, then we should be acting in line with how we think heaven would be like. We should be working to do our very best to have God's will done here in our lives.

We were all born with an intuition of God's existence and a knowing that heaven is a real place. Many have hardened their hearts over the years and now believe there is no God nor heaven or hell.

But just like we see the different birds and animals, how they build nests and migrate in different places at different times of the seasons, they have been given a God knowing what to do and when to do it. It is fascinating to watch and these things are undeniable.

He has given us an understanding of what is right and wrong. He has given us a conscience that helps us to discern when we are getting off into things that are out of the will of God. The bible states that God has put the commandments in our hearts to either accuse us or excuse us. It's the check and balance that keeps us from going in the wrong direction.

Romans 2:15
...the work of the law written in their hearts,
their conscience also bearing witness,
and between themselves their thoughts accusing
or else excusing them

Adam and Eve received this conscience after they ate of the tree that they were instructed not to partake of. That tree was called "The tree of the knowledge of good and evil". Once they ate the fruit of that tree, this conscience immediately kicked in and revealed in their spirits that they did wrong and they felt condemned. It wasn't God's initial plan but a backup just in case man was disobedient. That built-in condemnation drives us to repentance and to seek forgiveness with our Maker.

When a person keeps doing what they know is wrong to do and continues in it, then their heart begins to harden. Once their heart hardens, then their conscience no longer has that voice in their life to keep them from sinning and doing foolish things.

Look what it states here:

1 Timothy 4:2
speaking lies in hypocrisy,
having their own conscience seared with a hot iron

When a person's conscience has been seared with a hot iron, they become numb to things and now lack the awareness of the wrong they are committing. They speak lies in hypocrisy with no regret.

They begin to do things that are not rational and they do not seem to understand how off they sound. Their behavior has changed and no one seems to be able to change them through logical dialog.

It's like a person that stole a bike. The first time he did it, it bothered him for a while. But then he did it again and then again, and as he kept violating his conscience, he now robs grocery stores. His heart is hardened and now it has become a way of life.

DISCERNING

When you understand that God's will is for things down here to be like it is in heaven, then it's pretty easy to discern the ones that are not following His will.

Most people are not following His will, but many are in direct defiance of His will and plans. They are vehemently pushing back against anything or anyone that remotely has conservative and godly values.

Many of the Democrats and liberals have gone extreme in their ways, and I believe many of their consciences have no voice to harness their lies and deceptions any longer. Many have continued their radical left agendas and kept pressing for things they knew were not God's will.

Now we all have sinned and do need a Savior, but many have been on a rampage to eradicate God from everything in this country. We see this around the globe as well.

You can spot these groups fairly easily because their agendas are always anti-god. They act as if they walk in love but just try to get in their way and they will bite your head off. Their agendas have a sense of peace and unity but operate in selfishness and unrighteousness practice.

They use tactics that forces their will on others by mobs and riots and they follow lust, instead of love and are unaware of it.

HEART CHANGE

A heart cannot be changed on its own. People try to change their lifestyles to become a better person or sustain from eating certain foods to feel like their sacrifice is perfecting them. But that is just placating the flesh and doesn't have any real power to change the heart issue.

Religion only addresses our flesh but doesn't address the heart of a man. Religion says to do this and do that and then you are made right. That just makes us feel better for a moment, but deep down we know we have a heart issue and need a real experience with God.

As we saw in chapter six, we all walked according to the prince of the power of the air, but let's look at what it says in the verse after that:

Ephesians 2:3
among whom also we all once conducted ourselves in the lusts of our flesh, fulfilling the desires of the flesh and of the mind, and were by nature children of wrath, just as the others.

It says by nature we were all children of wrath. The Bible explains that we were born into this world with a sin nature that was passed on through Adam's sin.

Let's look at the behavior of a child to prove this out. Every child born, even though they are cute, is selfish in nature. They will cry until they get their milk, food, toy, and their way. They don't care much about anyone except themselves. We have to teach them to share their toys with other children because they naturally are selfish and need to be explained how to love and share. Even after repeatedly reprimanding them, we have to continue to help them to do right.

As a child gets older, they will continue to be selfish in certain areas of their life. And as adults, people are still trying to harness their feelings towards others every day.

And then many use religion as a means to atone for their sins.

People join a church and do good things to try to atone for their sin nature. But that is just putting a band aid on the problem and not addressing the real issue.

When Adam and Eve sinned, they ran and made a covering with fig leaves to hide their sin and shame. In a sense, that's what religion does. It just hides the problem.

When one understands their state and admits that they are a sinner, it's then that they know they need a real experience with God Himself. And at that moment, when they reach out to God for forgiveness through His Son Jesus, His Spirit comes into them and so does His nature as well. That's right; God's nature also comes into them.

Their sin nature is gone and that person now has God's nature. Like I said earlier, a book could be written on each one of these subjects. Much could be said, but when a person has received His Spirit and nature, they now have to learn how to love like God and live like God.

That person now needs to find out from the Bible who he or she is now and how to walk like God. It doesn't mean you won't be selfish any longer, but as a person renews their mind with the Word of God, it says they will be transformed.

Romans 12:2
And do not be conformed to this world,
but be transformed by the renewing of your mind...

This renewing is a process and the Church should be disciplining the believers to know Him and to live like Him.

ON EARTH AS IT IS IN HEAVEN

God has given us promises from His Word that if we have faith in them, then we can partake of heaven down here on earth.

The Bible is broken down into the Old Testament and the New Testament. The word "testament" means someone's will. God has left us a will and inheritance and not too many people know about it. If you don't know of an inheritance that someone left for you, then you usually won't partake of it.

Take a look at this Scripture. It explains that an inheritance doesn't go into effect until the testator dies. This is specifically speaking of Jesus the Testator leaving us an inheritance after His death.

> **Hebrews 9:16-17**
> For where there is a testament, there must also of necessity be the death of the testator. For a testament is in force after men are dead, since it has no power at all while the testator lives.

After His death, His will, or testament, went into effect and was left for us to receive and enjoy. We have to inquire about it and find out what blessings He has left for us to enjoy.

This might sound too good to be true, but Jesus tells us that His Father is taking everything that Jesus has and has declared it to us.

> **John 16:14-15**
> He will glorify Me, for He will take of what is Mine and declare it to you. All things that the Father has are Mine. Therefore I said that He will take of Mine and declare it to you.

As I learned the Scriptures, I found out that healing was part of my inheritance. I knew people in heaven were living in health, so God must have supplied health here on earth for us. He said on earth as it is in heaven, so He had to make it available for us to walk in health here.

We also know it's His will because we always see Jesus healing people throughout the gospels and we never see Him inflicting any disease or hurting anyone.

When He died on the cross and took away our sins, He also took away our sickness as well! Look at this Scripture below and see how He not only provided us eternal life to those that believe in Him but health as well in the here and now!

Matthew 8:17
that it might be fulfilled which was spoken by Isaiah the prophet, saying: "He Himself took our infirmities and bore our sicknesses."

While Jesus was being crucified on the cross, His Father put the punishment for all the sins of the world on Him. He was taking the full brunt and penalty for us. He was a sacrifice for our sins.

God could not use just anyone to take away our sins. It had to be a perfect sacrifice. The Jews would sacrifice a lamb annually, and its blood would make atonement and cover their sins. This lamb took the punishment for them. It had to be a lamb without a spot or blemish, which meant the lamb, in a sense, had no sin.

The promise for the Jewish people was that God was sending a Savior to take away their sins. He would be their Messiah.

When John the Baptist saw Jesus coming to the Jordan River to be baptized, he said, "Behold the lamb of God who takes away the sin of the world."

An amazing visitation from God's Son right there in the midst of them. Many saw Him as a great prophet that did great signs and wonders among them.

Many loved to listen to Him teach and preach the Word with power and authority. But unfortunately, many did not believe and esteem Him as their Messiah that would take away their sins.

He also received a brutal beating before He was crucified. If you have ever seen movies like The Passion of the Christ that shows His crucifixion, then you would know how they took a whip and struck Him many times on His body. The Bible states that He was unrecognizable after the Romans were done with Him.

But here is the good news. When He was beaten by the Romans, He was providing healing for our bodies. That's right, healing for our bodies now!

Look what Peter wrote for us to see:

> **1 Peter 2:24**
> who Himself bore our sins in His own body on the tree, that we, having died to sins, might live for righteousness—by whose stripes you were healed.

I hope you are seeing this. It states that He bore our sins and by the stripes or whips, we were healed. Here is another Scripture that Isaiah the prophet was inspired to write about the Messiah:

> **Isaiah 53:5**
> But He was wounded for our transgressions, He was bruised for our iniquities; The chastisement for our peace was upon Him, And by His stripes we are healed.

This might seem unfair that He paid the price for us like that but nevertheless, we personally have to believe these things that He did and then you too can have eternal life and walk in divine health as well.

Look what Jesus said at the last supper:

> **1 Corinthians 11:24**
> and when He had giving thanks, He broke it and said, "Take, eat; this is My body which is broken for you; do this in remembrance of Me"

Notice He said His body was broken for us and that we should be remembering what He did all the time. This lines up with the Scriptures we just read. He took our infirmities and bore our sicknesses.

I have lived in divine health for years, have prayed for scores of people, and have seen many healed of all sorts of diseases. Some had stage four cancers and were completely healed without any medications or any other remedies. Tumors dissolved away right there before us and many others healed of all types of illnesses.

He wants each and every one of us to find out about the wonderful inheritance and life He has left us here to enjoy.

He said it Himself, "Thy will be done on earth as it is in heaven."

CHAPTER 9

TIES TO ISRAEL

OVER THE YEARS, WE have seen so much anti-Semitism from many different groups and individuals that desire to harm the Jewish people. Just recently on October 27, 2018, eleven people were killed for just going to their temple. The gunman repeatedly said, "All Jews must die."

That night on the news, I remember a reporter saying that she thought we would have gotten over anti-Semitism by now. She didn't understand why these things were happening and that it boggles her mind.

Unfortunately, we will never see the end of anti-Semitism. It will always be with us here on earth. I know that's a hard statement, but it's just a fact of life.

Louis Farrakhan calls Hitler a great man and spews hateful speeches against Israel all the time. Where does this hatred for the Jewish people come from?

Why was Hitler so obsessed to extinguish every Jew on the planet? Putting innocent people in ovens and letting thousands just starve to death as they slowly turned into skeletons. How could this have happened? Why the rage?

Why are the Arab nations always eyeing Israel and looking to take them down. Iran has declared that their mission is to annihilate Israel off the map. It seems that Iran's sole existence is to build their nuclear warheads to destroy the Jewish people.

Let's see if we can look back in history and tie things together so we can understand some of the reasons for the behavior we are exhibiting. I pray that you will be able to comprehend what the Scriptures are showing us as I explain.

AN IMPORTANT HISTORY LESSON

God called Abraham out to a land that He would give to his ancestors years later. He told Abraham to walk over the land that I tell you. That land later would be the Promised Land, where Moses would lead the children of Israel out of Egypt and journey to possess the land God promised Abraham.

Many tribes over the years have tried to take back the land God promised them. They were constantly being harassed by one tribe or another. The Bible is filled with stories of their many battles that they encountered.

Satan used Pharaoh and other leaders to put the children of Israel in bondage or to death. Satan has always been able to find willing vessels to yield to his outlandish plans.

When you look into the Bible, you will find that Israel always had conflicts, not because they were troublemakers but because they were God's chosen people. Getting that one revelation will open a major door of understanding about what we see playing out at the United Nations and on the world platform.

Look at all the nations coming against Israel to take their land away. It's pretty amazing to see in the news how they are so laser focused on taking back Israel's land.

Why don't they just leave them alone? Their property is like the size of New Jersey. They're not bothering anyone. They are a very peaceable people yet you would never think that with all the lying accusations that they receive. Let's look even deeper, if possible, to show some more specifics.

When Abraham was old, he only had menservants but had no sons or offspring to fulfill the promise God gave him. So God told him when he was in his eighties to have a son with his wife Sarah. They tried but to no avail. So instead of continuing to believe what God had spoken, Sarah came up with a new idea and told Abraham to just lie with her maidservant

Hagar and have a child with her. So he did and she gave birth to a son and they named him Ishmael.

But later, God told Abraham that Ishmael would not be the son that He promised, for Abraham accomplished this in his own strength through Hagar the maidservant. God told him that he would have a son through Sarah who now was about ninety years of age. Wow, what a promise and Abraham was about a hundred years old.

Well, they believed God and Sarah became pregnant and gave birth to a son and they named him Isaac. Isaac would carry on the legacy of his father and have two sons. One of the sons was named Jacob. Jacob's name was changed to Israel who gave birth to the twelve sons which would later become the leaders of the twelve tribes of Israel.

So, I've very quickly explained how God brought about the children of Israel.

Now, do you remember Ishmael? He grew and became great and his offspring multiplied. The Bible tells us that Ishmael's offspring are the Arab people that we know of today. The same offspring, for the most part, that have been persecuting Israel and trying to destroy them.

Now the children of Ishmael, who consist of the Arab people and the children of Israel, all came from the same father. That's right; Abraham is the father of them all. They are half-brothers and they are constantly at war with one another.

They both have the same natural father and many can't seem to get along together for a moment.

Here is a Scripture that shows us that this isn't just some family feud that we are witnessing, but this is a spiritual feud for sure.

> **Galatians 4:29**
> But, as he who was born according to the flesh then persecuted him who was born according to the Spirit, even so it is now.

This is exactly what we are seeing before our eyes. The person here in the Scripture that is born according to the flesh is Ishmael. He was born naturally through Hagar.

Isaac was born according to the Spirit, which was when Abraham believed God and Isaac his son was born according to God's promise.

That verse was written about two thousand years ago and states that Ishmael's children would persecute Isaac's children. It tells us what has been happening all these years and what is happening today.

PERSECUTION

Anyone that comes out of Israel shall be persecuted because darkness is working against Abraham's offspring.

Here is a huge revelation to understand.

Israel's Messiah would come through Abraham's offspring and guess Who that might be? You guessed it, Jesus!

He would be born and be a sacrifice to make atonement for their sins. Satan was well aware of the Scriptures, and he knew that the Christ would be born through Abraham's offspring and in the town of Bethlehem.

So when Jesus was born, Satan looked for someone he could use to take Him down. Satan has been using people whenever he can to persecute and destroy the people of God.

And as we see from Scripture, Satan used Herod the king to try to take His life at an early age. Herod had every child in Bethlehem put to death from two years and under, but God warned Joseph, His father, in a dream to get out of Bethlehem.

Matthew 2:13
...behold, an angel of the Lord appeared to Joseph in a dream, saying, "Arise, take the young Child and His mother, flee to Egypt, and stay there until I bring you word; for Herod will seek the young Child to destroy Him."

So Satan was unsuccessful but made many attempts to have Him killed along the way.

We see at the Last Supper how Satan used Judas to betray Jesus for money that the religious leaders had promised him. Satan will work through our sinful nature and unrighteous ideologies.

> **John 13:2**
> And supper being ended, the devil having already put it into the heart of Judas Iscariot, Simon's son to betray Him.

No money is worth yielding to darkness and fulfilling Satan's desires. I'm sure most wouldn't do it if they only knew what was happening behind the scenes.

We even see Paul the Apostle being used by this prince of darkness before he became a believer. He tried to have Christians destroyed beyond measure.

> **Galatians 1:13**
> For you have heard of my former conduct in Judaism, how I persecuted the church of God beyond measure and tried to destroy it.

Jesus told His disciples that they too would be persecuted as well as those that would follow after Him.

Jesus said:

> **John 15:20**
> Remember the word that I said to you, "A servant is not greater than his master." If they persecuted Me, they will also persecute you.

This is not a natural thing that people would go after others like this. This is a spiritual thing that has been going on for thousands of years. That's why anti-Semitism isn't going away.

The media and our society reports everything as natural, which I do understand why, but it leaves the rest with one side of the story. Many things are tied back to Israel and most people do not realize it.

Anyone associated with Israel and Jesus is a target for experiencing persecution.

Because President Trump stands for Israel, believes in Jesus, and pushes godly agendas, this is the main root cause for all this resistance we are watching. It's not what the liberals and media say it is. This goes all the way back to Israel.

THE OUTSIDER

Satan had Jesus crucified by the hands of the Pharisee and Scribes. Why did they yield to this horrible thing? For one thing, they didn't want to be found out what a bunch of hypocrites they were and then end up losing their fine estates and lavish living.

Satan will use our lusts and desires to manipulate us to do things for him. When we operate out of fear and selfishness, we will do whatever it takes to keep from losing our stuff.

Look what the religious leaders said:

> **John 11:47-48**
> Then the chief priests and the Pharisees gathered a council and said, "What shall we do? For this Man works many signs. If we let Him alone like this, everyone will believe in Him, and the Romans will come and take away both our place and nation."

You would have thought that they would have embraced Him and would have wanted to learn how to work miracles like Him. But instead, these religious leaders said Jesus was of the Devil and that He had a demon. When you're all about yourself, you'll end up making outrageous statements.

They were more concerned with their power and greed than the wonderful signs from heaven they were experiencing. And this is how Satan was able to use them to destroy the Son of God.

The Scribes and Pharisee threw Jesus under the bus so to speak and set up false accusations and fake news against Him. Fake news has been around since time began.

They evidently were able to get the people to actually shout "crucify Him" even after all He had done for them. It shows us how lies can influence a society in such a powerful way – even capable of bringing down the Son of God.

We should be appalled of all the lies and fake stories that are being broadcasted across our country but not surprised. It's unfortunately having a negative effect on our generation.

A SIDE NOTE

Jesus laid down His life and allowed them to take Him down.

Isaiah 53:7
He was oppressed and He was afflicted,
Yet He opened not His mouth;
He was led as a lamb to the slaughter,
And as a sheep before its shearers is silent,
So He opened not His mouth.

We see He didn't open His mouth to try to talk Herod out of having Himself condemned and crucified. Jesus knew it was His Father's will to be put to death and pay the price for the sins of the world.

Satan thought he had done a great thing, but it boomeranged on him big time! He didn't realize how this was going to make a way for all those that would believe in Him and receive the forgiveness for their sins.

We see that most of the religious leaders didn't care about God or the people but just about their little old selves. They spoke eloquent long prayers while dressed in their long robes, proclaiming to love God.

Look what Jesus said about these men:

Luke 20:45-47
Then, in the hearing of all the people, He said to His disciples, "Beware of the scribes, who desire to go around in long robes, love greetings in the marketplaces, the best seats in the synagogues, and the best places at feasts, who devour widows' houses, and for a pretense make long prayers. These will receive greater condemnation."

Look what it says in John chapter 12:

John 12:43
for they loved the praise of men more than the praise of God.

Like many politicians, they will claim to love our nation and people but have more love for control and power. Many love to be seen and adorned by men instead of doing what's right for the American people.

THE DC MACHINE

When Donald Trump first announced that he was going to drain the swamp, most didn't know what that meant. It sounded like a catchy phrase though. But the corrupt politicians of Washington knew exactly what he meant. They immediately started to scramble to figure out what they were going to do with this outsider.

Who is this one interfering with our way of doing things? Will he be able to convince the American people that we are not who we say we are? Will this outsider expose our hypocrisy and cause us to lose our credibility with the people?

Will we lose our place of authority and positions that we so dearly love? This outsider speaks of law and order. Our crimes will be exposed. He needs to be stopped at all costs. The stakes are high and something must be done to overturn this outsider.

Most Americans were unaware of the swamp and deep state, which was entrenched underground where no one could detect or identify its comings and goings.

Most of the American people now see things in a much different light today much due to the hard investigative work by a few good people. They have been able to slowly expose the many ruthless deeds they had plotted to take down the president and overturn our democracy.

And just like the religious leaders who were used by Satan to take down Jesus for the love of greed and power, so we see the same by some of the politicians and leaders of our day.

CHAPTER 10

DON'T FALL ASLEEP, AMERICA

IF THE MAJORITY OF the American people will stand up for the rule of law and for our constitution, we will continue to maintain the freedoms and opportunities that so many people from around the world seek to come here for.

God help us if we sleep on the job and allow these ungodly agendas to run rampant and reign over our society. America will fall into big government, socialism, bankruptcy, and collapse from within if we do not continue in our Founding Father's framework.

We need to fight for the American way and not allow this great nation to be turned over into the hands of a deep state! Too many of our great patriarchs and soldiers have given their lives and have died for this nation that stands for liberty and justice. Let it not be in vain!

The president is plowing through the swamplands of Washington D.C. in his chariot and exposing the deep state, which is camouflaged in the weeds and imbedded in the thick, muddy waters.

Let us keep supporting like-minded men and women like him that hold the values of justice and truth so we can continue to see America prosper and thrive for generations to come.

The ones that are resisting our president from accomplishing the things that are dear to his heart are not really hurting the president as they think they are. But they're actually hindering blessings to flow down onto the American people in who so many desperately need a better way of life.

If the president doesn't get all of the things that he desires to get done, the believers who are already aware of God's truth and provisions will do just fine either way, but it's the ones that do not know as of yet the nuts and bolts of what's going on.

I'm hopeful that the ones that are working against this president will turn to the Lord and follow His way and His agendas.

All of mankind is susceptible to Satan's ways, but we can keep ourselves from falling into his snares and traps by seeking after God and having a relationship with Him.

When you begin to seek God and His Word, then you won't be so easily hoodwinked and deceived. This cannot be an option for our lives; we need to learn His truth so we're not living for the wrong kingdom.

Jesus warned us that Satan is cunning and that he is working his wiles in the earth, so it's no wonder that our schools, media, government, and the family have been hijacked by this evil way. This did not happen by itself.

It's been methodically designed to divide and overturn every good society on the earth. Every nation is in jeopardy if their society becomes inundated with anti-god policies and agendas. They have to be kept in check or it spreads out of control.

As we discussed earlier, God's kingdom is working on the earth and it's His will for us to be living as if we were in heaven. Satan, however, is doing everything he can to not let that happen.

Jesus teaches in Matthew the twelfth chapter that Satan does have a kingdom that he runs here on the earth. But understand, these two kingdoms do not work hand in hand. They operate in complete opposite of one another.

After Jesus healed a man who was blind and mute, by casting out this devil, the religious leaders accused Jesus of healing him by the power of Satan. Jesus explained that He could not be of Satan's kingdom because one kingdom cannot heal the same person that it made sick. If that would happen, the kingdom would be divided and it could not stand.

Jesus said:

> **Matthew 12:26**
> If Satan casts out Satan, he is divided against himself. How then will his kingdom stand?

Many have said that God puts sickness on people to help make them a better person or even that He has taken people's lives with some kind of disease for His glory or whatever... NOT TRUE!

He just finished telling us that it's impossible for that to happen. People have made up their own doctrines to fit their unbiblical narratives. The reason we only see Jesus heal people and never hurt people is because that's all His kingdom will and can do or else it would not stand. And furthermore, heaven doesn't have any sickness to put on anyone, even if it wanted to.

Many people have turned their back on God because they were told that God was responsible for their loved one's challenges or death. What a tragedy to live life thinking the One that created you is against you.

Look what Paul stated here in Romans:

> **Romans 8:31**
> What then shall we say to these things?
> If God is for us, who can be against us?

God is there to help us if we are working for the right kingdom. He cannot assist us if we are acting contrary to truth and godliness. Most people live their lives the way they want to live it and then when they get in trouble, they expect immediate help from God. If He doesn't take care of all their problems within a few hours, then He either doesn't exist or they get mad at Him.

That is, unfortunately, the mentality of most Americans. They tried to get His help once and He didn't wave His magic wand over the situation and make it all go away. So then, we came up with a new theory of why He didn't take care of the problem or who knows, maybe He doesn't exist.

If we're honest and straightforward with Him, I believe we would see doors start to open and doors start to close on our behalf to rectify our problems.

If we would humble ourselves and go to Him with a right heart, He will surely be there for us.

He has even given us a host of angelic beings to work on our behalf as well. Satan is not the only one that has helpers doing his work. God's angels are greater in power and far more in number.

We see in these Scriptures that Jesus Himself received help from angels, so how much more assistance will we need when we run into difficulties in life?

> **Luke 22:40-43**
> When He came to the place, He said to them,
> "Pray that you may not enter into temptation."
> And He was withdrawn from them about a stone's
> throw, and He knelt down and prayed, saying,
> "Father, if it is Your will, take this cup away from Me;
> nevertheless not My will, but Yours, be done." Then an
> angel appeared to Him from heaven, strengthening Him.

An angel came and strengthened Him, but we're not sure exactly what he did that helped assist Him through that night. We know He was about to be separated from the Father and the sin of mankind was about to be poured on Him.

And then we see another time where He was fasting and being tempted by the Devil in the wilderness for forty days and forty nights. And after all the temptations, He was again helped by angels.

> **Mark 1:13**
> And He was there in the wilderness forty days,
> tempted by Satan, and was with the wild beasts;
> and the angels ministered to Him.

Here we see there was more than one angel that ministered to Him and so they might have brought Him some food, which we can see in another story in 1 Kings 19:1-8 that an angel brought Elijah the prophet a baked cake and a jar of water.

God has given us His Word that shows us He has already provided a supply for our future and help when we need it. We just need to find out His will and then trust that He will bring it to pass. He will lead us to live in victory and help us not to fear any longer. He has a wonderful plan for our lives and all we need to do is find out what He has in store for us!

Finding and doing His will brings the greatest joy you will ever experience. And working for His kingdom and fulfilling His plan has eternity rewards. He said to lay up treasures in heaven.

Look what it states in the Book of Matthew:

> **Matthew 6:19-21**
> lay up for yourselves treasures in heaven, where
> neither moth nor rust destroys and where thieves
> do not break in and steal. For where your treasure is,
> there your heart will be also.

Let's work with God and His kingdom and see our families, our communities, and the world thrive with godly values. Join the winning team, for the Bible tells us which kingdom overcomes and wins, so why waste any more time.

I pray that the truths from this book have helped you to see the dependency we need to have on God in our lives. Without His Word and guidance, we will be tossed to and fro with every wind of doctrine.

There is much to understand about each one of these subjects that we have uncovered, so move forward, have a real experience with God, and search out His will for your life.

Let's leave a legacy and run the race that is set before us!

Paul stated:

Philippians 3:13-14
Brethren, I do not count myself to have apprehended; but one thing I do, forgetting those things which are behind and reaching forward to those things which are ahead, I press toward the goal for the prize of the upward call of God in Christ Jesus.

ABOUT THE AUTHOR

JOHN FRASER has been a Bible teacher and a pastor for over seventeen years. He is dedicated to educating people on how God's kingdom works here on the earth and how to apply His principles to their everyday lives. He has two grown children, Tania and Jonathan, and resides with his wife Nancy in New York.

To contact, please write to:
Author John Fraser
P.O. Box 83
Amityville, N.Y. 11701